FORTY-SIX ADIRONDACK SONNETS

J. L. MARANVILLE

SAND PEBBLE PRESS

Sand Pebble Press 2005

Copyright 2005 by J.L. Maranville

D. Achilles Bellone
Design

ISBN:0-9771153-0-5

CONTENTS

An introductory Word	ii
MARSHALL	3
COUCHSACHRAGA	5
ALLEN	7
SEWARD	9
DONALDSON	11
EMMONS	13
SEYMOUR	15
PANTHER	17
SANTANONI	19
IROQUOIS	21
ALGONQUIN	23
WRIGHT	25
COLDEN	27
REDFIELD	29
GRAY	31
WHITEFACE	33
ESTHER	35
CASCADE	37
TABLETOP	39
PHELPS	41
PORTER	43
COLVIN	45
STREET & NYE	47
NYE & STREET (still)	49
DIAL	51
DIX	53

SAWTEETH	55
MACOMB	57
WOLFJAW (I)	59
NIPPLETOP	61
ROCKY PEAK RIDGE	63
GIANT	65
BIG SLIDE	67
SOUTH DIX	69
EAST DIX	71
SADDLEBACK	73
BASIN	75
WOLFJAW (II)	77
CLIFF	79
MARCY	81
GOTHICS	83
HOUGH	85
ARMSTRONG	87
SKYLIGHT	89
BLAKE	91
HAYSTACK	93
FORTY SIX NOTES	95
Some Suggested Reading	103
A Brief Afterword	105

An Introductory Word

The Adirondacks are to my mind man-made mountains. They were crafted by the early explorers, residents and writers who viewed them as a place. The Almighty Creator formed the sphere we inhabit and let Nature determine the surface. But the geological and geographical area we envision when we say the name Adirondacks took shape in the nineteenth century. The early guides -- the scientists -- the historians and writers -- the painters -- and the great tradition of photographers -- all had a role in shaping our thinking about the region. The High Peaks area especially has a presence within the larger forest preserve.

A special word is called for as regards the irrepressible Verplanck Colvin -- explorer, surveyor, enthusiast -- a man who saw them individually and whole. And his lifelong friend and assistant Mills Blake helped us see Colvin more clearly.

An often unsung group comprises the stalwart New Yorkers who live in the region. Numerous towns, villages and hamlets abound with people for whom the area is simply their village or home. I know a man who lives outside Warrensburg on 39 wooded acres and thinks it's getting too crowded.

There are many wonderful books about the Adirondacks, their history, their value and so forth. All the more valuable because the area will never be what is was. Would Whiteface happen today? It was not a given in the Thirties. The Adirondacks exist in a complex political environment. They have had and continue to have a dedicated cohort of good workers and users. They also continue to attract a fair number of passionate lovers. It is a great relationship.

In the poems in this volume, I have attempted to convey my feelings for and my thoughts about the Adirondacks.

In my walks, I have had the good fortune of being delighted by gems of thought expressed by various walkers ahead of me. I have felt free to carry them along and return them sprinkled throughout these sonnets. They have the miraculous quality of being in two places at once.

A special mention needs to be made about two writers working in different genres in different centuries. I was reading once again John Donne's *Holy Sonnets* at the same time I was engrossed in Russell Banks' *Cloudsplitter* a novel not quite centered in the Adirondacks, but Banks' sense of the region brings his narrative to life. Since I have all my life taken great pleasure in living near and in the Adirondacks, I wanted to give expression to my experience of them. In a sense the mountains all share a common form, but the forces that have wrought the variations expressed are ever at work. Donne and Banks set me to thinking. Forty Six Adirondack Sonnets grew from that thinking.

These sonnets are dedicated to all who have helped in the creation and preservation of the Adirondacks, and most especially to Arlene.

But now ask the beasts to teach you
 And the birds of the air to tell you,
Or the reptiles of the earth to instruct you
 And the fish of the sea to inform you.
Which of these does not know
 That the Hand of God has done this.
In this Hand is the soul of every living thing
 And the breath of all Mankind.

Job 12: 7 - 10

FORTY SIX ADIRONDACK SONNETS

MARSHALL

The fog sits patiently upon a sea
Of slopes cresting across an ever darker
Expanse reaching toward an ever vaguer
Horizon, white to grey, dim and hazy.

At the end of the wave, pressing the verge,
Similar on the surface to all the rest,
Discernible difference at the crest .
Out of sameness, identities emerge.

One among many revealing oneness.
A relative permanence within change.
Above the basic rock where unity
Prevails, forces create variety,
Welcome within an atmospheric range,
Offering again the lesson endless.

COUCHSACHRAGA

Along the reach of a cold, cold river
Long ago, moccasin prints set softly.
Eyes saw not dismal wilds but paths suggesting
The first and firm foundations of the earth.

Streams leaped and tumbled and skipped and rippled
Singing untutored in deep forest hollows.
Breezes raised clouds of leaves in narrow dells.
The buck brushed the green boughs with his antlers.

Lit by sky's candle, spruce rose in breathing
Silence. Struggling through the misty atmosphere
Sun and rain ripened the sweet fruit he found
Where the Great Spirit laid a hand in the midst.
Snow came and skins kept him warm in winter
On slopes covered with trees and filled with game.

ALLEN

Sun splashes and spills down a snowy slope
Bringing forth all light to where night's dark hue
Shaded by moon lit mix of gray and blue
Crystallized a crusted cold envelope.

What seems a silent stillness teems nocturnal
Hours with forest creatures feeding, still,
Scurrying across a shallow flowing rill
Falling amid flora and fauna diurnal.

Plashy rill continues its poised descent
Plowing, slowing, spreading as it traces
The contours through the changing population
Of plants and animals whose habitation
Is nourished as the streaming water races
To become one with sparkling Opalescent.

SEWARD

Dark sky. Bright sky. Flashing sky. Booming sky.
Rumbling sky. Crackling sky. Banging sky.
Shivering light. Pale light. Startling light.
Black. White. Gray. Spreading far away. Suddenly

Streaking straight through tree tops, fuel to sustain
Blazing canopy. Striking duff again
Sending groping flame through roots burning bright.
Crack. Boom. Bang. No mercy. No gentle rain.

Blaze dying, fluttering, suddenly climb
Licking trunk, leaping, hopping limb to limb
Sending smoke skyward, reddening the night.
Burning blowdown. Burning standing timber.

Insatiable flame eating forest flesh,
Leaving orts of charred stumps and endless ash.

DONALDSON

Torrent. Tons of sheeting water, swelling streams.
Sweeping, first, small grains of sand and spindly
Flora sprung from silty soil. No kindly
Gentle brook. Tumbling mountain side teems

With raging rush tearing at root and rock,
All the while spreading, surging, careening,
Edging outward, seeping under to unlock
Long accumulated earth, loosening

Until, from below a rumble shoulders
Up the mountain's side with tremors further
Shaking loose bigger and bigger boulders,
Breaking free and falling, faster, farther.
Water, soil, silva in a slashing tide -
Violence yielding a spectacular slide.

EMMONS

At the edge, the verge, the outer limit
Looking past lake upon comely lake, you know
The last of day's sun seen from your summit
Above the abyss. Clouds gather below.

Criss-crossing your slopes tangle upon tangle,
Fallen trunks, spring thickets of young balsam,
Birch and more birch. Thousands of snags dangle
At restive angles, not one of them plumb.

This jungle of saplings where birch flourish
Assures a chaste canopy after blowdown,
Nature's curse and vibrant promise, and vests
New rooted verdurous growth to nourish
Mountain ash to start and sturdy spruce to crown
Again this intrepid corner of the crests.

SEYMOUR

Wind. Strong wind. Stiff Wind. Stiffer and stronger
Blowing. Blowing. Blowing hard against trunks
Breaking, busting, crashing, crushing smaller
Trunks under century-old deep rooted trunks.

Blowing. Blowing thick limbs, rock loosening
All soil, all roots resist but not withstand it.
Driving water — horizontal — leveling,
Lifting forest. Scouring against granite.

But that was more than five decades ago.
Soil settled. Seeds spread, found sufficient moisture
To sprout and grow. As tiny roots took hold
Small Birch, sheltering flora, began to grow
As nursing canopy for spruce and fir.
Hurricane had its day, but mountain held.

PANTHER

Delicate, shapely prints pressing cleanly
The crusted snow, whitening in the dawn,
Clustered at lush sedges, then suddenly
Surefooted leaps diagonally down

The slope, along the black and milky stream
Flowing to the foot, freshening a pond
On whose surface floats a mound, it would seem,
A domicile devised with sticks and mud.

Elsewhere large paw prints encircle a spruce
Leaning against a ledge, dry and protected.
While high up twig ends, chewed and gnawed hang loose,
Tiny tunnels get nosily inspected.

As danger circles slowly overhead,
Nocturnal browsers amble off to bed.

SANTANONI

Across the clustered, tree-hidden tonsure
Quiet, almost chant-like, floats a symphony
Of gentle vespers in a verdant cloister
Cloaking earth and heaven in harmony.

The world is far from too much with us here.
A brief while dynamite blast and engine roar
Ventured fast upon this sanctuary
Like cannon shot at some old monastery,
Until the impulse that sought mineral
Riches surrendered to a deeper appeal.

Now girdled with maples, beech, and black cherry,
A monks cloth splotched with ponds strung out like beads,
Refuge for the seeker solitary,
Where contemplation substitutes for deeds.

IROQUOIS

The tops of trees harden on cold mountain face,
Successors to survivors of long past
Wintry storms that brought across the ages blast
Smoothing centuries sculpting work in steep place.

Sunlight and shadow parcel the visible
Crest as the pristine mountain could not make
Up its mind and thus spilled for Janus' sake
Its beauty down each slope in tender tumble.

Autumn brilliance spreads a colorful grace
Moving with the hours carrying warm
Against the grey dark's cold and frosty grip,
Inching skyward, reaching hip upon hip,
Tree by tree, rock by rock and fern by fern
Slowly up the mountainside's yielding face.

ALGONQUIN

Rising from among a string of summits,
Peaks abreast of peaks, shoulder to shoulder,
Ever steeper, boulder after boulder,
Stepping stones round hanging cliffs that plummet

As an eternity captured in a thought.
A granite face pitches through the open space
Till trees again have root and find a place
To cling and hold in crevice barely caught.

All is present in your elemental
Composition. Fallen trees, trickling water
Wearing stone away from bigger stones beneath.
Decomposition is as fundamental
To your vital being as is matter
To the beauty of your many graced wreath.

WRIGHT

Seldom a destination, a detour
Along the way, but one most choose to make.
But not all chose. Some, whom lofty life did take
Crashing through needled limbs in a fateful hour,

Came unseeking, nevertheless found rest
Beneath the canopy unexpected,
Splattered across a grave, not neglected,
Of timbered slope and rock beneath the crest.

Grand headstone. While at their feet still cascade
Sweet waters and break upon spattered mosses
That softly heighten boulders mostly buried.
Silver streak across the sky that carried
Them still scattered here, their spirits still possess
This peak though their bones someplace else are laid.

COLDEN

Exposed and naked rock, slides showing scar
With huge flanks holding fast, a sprawling rampart
Shields deep wooded valleys, rugged stalwart,
Great walls rising near perpendicular.

Not a mere bulwark, but vital station,
Resolute adjuvant of sturdiness
And stability for ranges east and west,
Ancient and vigilant centurion

At the pass. Imposing rock face plummets
To cold deep waters precious to the flow
Of lake to brook to lake to brook to river
Gathering steadily to deliver
Over opalescent feldspar far below
The iridescent trickle at the summit.

REDFIELD

Sun. Solar light. Mid-morn white, blazing, bright
Bright azure sky. Clouds high, clouds small, clouds still,
Scattered. Remote from summit and from hidden rill,
Dulcet, Lilliputian fellows in flight.

Summits under the sun. Basking. Warming.
Distant, but not too, moving beams caress
Shining limbs and branches rendered seamless,
Sloping steeply, dappled valley forming.

Stillness reigns across the peaks this morning.
Barely breeze enough to sough through upper
Limbs. Thousand-starred brook water's tumbling run
Sends swelling, piano sound ascending
From bleached and polished stones, breaking over,
Carrying, sustaining life under the sun.

GRAY

Vigilant beside the kingdom's jewel,
Bound in fealty like chivalrous laws,
Not unlike, in loyalty, old Lear's fool,
Grounded in the majesty of Tahawus.

Determined to deter all invasion
Shored with massive rock, rifts, and walled ravine,
Spreading sturdy spruce against erosion,
Holding chill ooze and rills and springs unseen.

Cavernous rocks and gurgling water
Captured as icy drizzle of a cloud
Gathered on trees, lichen grown and gray with years.
To the reach of the stream bank there is naught or
Barely a broken twig rarely allowed. Proud
Northwall to the sanctity of Heaven's tears.

WHITEFACE

Supple slopes rising from a serene shore,
Softly contoured crest with snow-capped arête
Enchanting, through each season's rich allure,
Thousands passing along your silhouette.

Gracefully arcing, sloping western shoulder,
A gentle undulation that smoothes over
With forest fabric woven trees that cover
Rugged weathered, helter skelter boulder.

Northeast winds work against a granite face
Presented to the valley coddling,
Along coursing waters of AuSable,
Beauty, most invaded, to enable
Dignity, undiminished, welcoming
Like an apron'd grandmother to her place.

ESTHER

Sky frozen slopes indivisibly white
Unmoving, frigorific, yielding change,
Motion visible in a flurry bright
Against the darkness of the nearest range.

Falling gently, opaline, watchable,
Whitening deeply and more deeply summit,
Slope, stone and flora green, grey and sable,
Blind unity, delicate and dulcet.

Unreplicated instances of beauty
Indistinguishable, yet no two alike,
Glittering in seeming solidarity,
Crystals reigning fair, flake by patient flake.
Wind, sun and shade create disparity
Sculpting graceful forms that green tomorrows make.

CASCADE

For many you proffered the first sweet taste,
A promise of transport easily taken
Through rugged plants, maple, beech and oaken
Brushing by unnoticed bunchberry in haste.

Scrambling feet moving with legerity past
Conifer and birch, boulder and bracken,
Striding toward the sky breathlessly driven
Pulled ever summitward until at last…

Until, until, until standing among
Fragile alpine plants under azure lustrous,
Bald rock becomes the pungent porch of God.
Descending leisurely as trillium nod,
Striding around deer hair and cushioned moss,
Steps timed to cascading waters winsome song.

TABLETOP

Soft stroking balsam filling fragrant space,
Between the blowdown trunk and broken branch
Narrow animal trails traverse and advance
Across depressions shallow under spruce,

Faint evidence in damp soil of unseen
Presences of residence unrevealed
By covering cripplebush's concealed
Holding watch against growing balsam's green.

Above the rising ground conifers dense
Dominate the wrinkled unkempt plateau
Like a scruffy rug that offers no show
Of the gradual elevations hence

Where subtle shifts in tapered trees belie
A summit softly slumbering nearby.

PHELPS

Chemical elements and physical
Forces were all it took to bring about
In time almost immeasurable no doubt
This surface that rises, falls, rhythmical.

Simple thawing and freezing did the feat
Driving the primal rock smashing and crashing
A path toward the sun, then turning and grinding
Everything in its great scraping retreat

Ungraspable. The scale, the depth, the duration
We learn in awe from the theorizer
Who studies the evidence, the debris,
How this small plot, this singular formation
Came to be. But how odd. How is not why we're
Blessed with this, our, "heaven up-h'isted country."

PORTER

Ever present to the townsfolk, a form
Bright in the morning sun, standing duty,
A comfortable silhouette against a storm,
Catching them unawares with unsought beauty

Undeniable for a moment , then
Viewed as one of many, ordinary,
Familiar, easily within their ken
The whole collegium extraordinary.

From time to time, at work or passing by
Or often pausing at a neighbor's gate,
Folks will chat about the weather, view the sky,
Survey the changing leaves and speculate,
And somehow moved, recognize with inward eye
For each of them the mountain's their estate.

COLVIN

Water seeps and wells in uncertain motion,
Trickling over rock and root, building
Into a stream, slowed by a stillwater,
Joined to others, guided by nature's hand
Through bends and turns, becoming a river
Flowing over falls and past towns, serving
The people on its way to the ocean.

Also on summits seeping through men's packs
Welled an idea, spilling and splashing,
Slipping and sliding outward from its source,
Trap diked granite like deep within the mind,
Flowing over doubts, driven by a force
Through chiseled halls. Grasping nature's blessing,
The people created the Adirondacks.

STREET & NYE

Grudging boundary crouching in between
Eastern and Western regions rising like
A humped purgatory of peaks holding
Demon thorns of crowns of hidden blowdown
Sloping acres of deadfall and debris
Thick and dreadful, a grim monotony
Of trees and bushes.. no easy street is nigh.

For all that a forest of spruce and balsam
Continuous cover — a fragrant quilt
Whose comfort made more welcome as its patches
Spread across clean duff and fresh bunchberry
All the lovelier for its suddenness
Sprung up amid soft moss and tufts of grass.

Branched left and right, north and south, not natural
Designations but merely useful guides
For stragglers with the forest foreign.

NYE & STREET still

Fox and toad, skunk and snake need not such terms
To make their way direct. To them you have
No name nor need for one -- or even two.
Their trails branch not for summits sake to see.
They ramble neath the bramble never lost.

Thrush and sparrow, chickadee and vireo
All know their range and navigate within
To forage for their food they fly full speed
Ahead straight in their intended direction
Never confused never turned and twisted
Fully at ease in their leafy habitation.

Never knowing the relief of sighting the lodge.

DIAL

When's a summit a summit? Who's to say?
North? South? Some lower, some higher, one the same.
What's in a name? Who marks the time of day?
Beauty's beauty for all that. Keep your name.

Often you're simply a stop for those heading
To Nippletop. Yet bright partridgeberry
And Indian pipe popping up and spreading
In your duff as other's seem as merry.

Maiden hair, hay scented, bublet and fragrant
Ferns all flourish and whorls of sheep sorrel
Along your wooded slopes bloom luxuriant
And a vetch is yet a vetch. No quarrel..

Four-thousand-twenty's four-thousand-twenty,
But only one's a summit! We must have plenty.

DIX

Mountain deep in the midst of aged mountains
Your majesty furthers forth in forested slope,
Inviting our fleeting steps in lasting hope
We recognize the riches of our domain,

Prompting a melioristic impulse
Faintly felt at first as part of pleasure,
Planted within that we may come to treasure
Our fragile connection with all things else.

Power divine despite our weakness dared ordain
That we, as price for pleasure, should protect
Not only fragile lily and scurrying hare
But also scabrous granite and growling bear
Against all senseless waste, and ne'er neglect
A sacred trust placed on strength uncertain.

SAWTEETH

Vertical rock face. Vertical rack face.
Vertical rock face rough ripping the sky,
Your series of serrations sets a pace
Past cedars and pines at landings that lie

Along the silhouette, imposing ledge
Against the limitless blue, wave after wave
Blurring the soft green cedar like a hedge
Holding and hiding nature's rough crude grave.

More often viewed than climbed your peaks alone
Face fire, sleeting water, wind stiff rods
Challenging perception and legs worn raw.
Not what I see, the native viewer saw
Gigantic stone stair steps trod by cloudy gods;
Long before manufactured steel was stone.

MACOMB

Languid legs dangling downward to spread toes
That touch old Elk nestled among the peaks
Giving birth to a trickling Boquet
That carries tiny sands to St. Laurent.

From soft moss to rigid root held carpet
Rocks and boulder break and burst on surface
Sometimes clear of low growth brush and bracken
Against an aged wall of veined granite

Looming larger, somehow steeper. Suddenly
An egregious gash, widely ripped and slashed,
A dazzling, tempting, dizzying slide.
Smaller spruce cling, kept stunted by windy
Storms that rage, flash and Alpine flora lash,
Then sun drenched glistening as storms subside.

WOLF JAW (I)

Your flower petals, lichen, moss and trees
Grow similar to those of all your fellows.
Your varied greens and browns and reds and yellows
Appropriate our senses as they please.

Our brains seek — crave — a pattern that will ease
The complexity we perceive, and bestow
A recognition of mountain clues that grow
To form a confection that our mind's eye sees.

Your ridges, your cols, and your slabrous slope
Seduce and manipulate our senses
Till we draw plant filled contours and make dense
The empty spaces of our mental map.

At your trailhead we imagine — we saw
With summit fever in our brain —wolf jaw.

NIPPLETOP

Ridge after ridge rising into the sky
Make it easy to miss the loveliness
That lies along ribs within the quietness
Of ferns in patchwork pleasing to the eye.

The long wall of the range is standing by
To draw attention as it dwarfs the less
In stature but not in advancing freshness.
The simple striped maple has its beauty.

Below the bulk's soaring, shapely swelling
Dwell sturdy bracken beside the pebbly bourne,
The slightly hidden, almost forbidden
Flora abloom beneath the abdomen.
Ahead, ascendant, appearing in turn
The breast, abruptly unveiled... breathtaking.

ROCKY PEAK RIDGE

Sand pebble and limy silt compaction
Move hot iron and silicon to thrust
Sediment and metamorphic tension
Folding and compressing from core to crust.

Mineral matter from an ancient sea,
Molten magmas rising through the mantle,
Blocks of crumpling crust, shoving, shearing free,
Born as melt, finally feldspar domical.

Invaders from the surging arctic slid
Across the Grenville structure polishing,
Plucking as they pulled back, frozen rivers
Carving cirques, gouging, tossing boulders scattered,
Leaving crystal streams sparkling, rocks shining,
Built on the drip,drip, drip of a billion years.

GIANT

Dark dikes decorate the bedrock scabrous.
Beyond the base face scrub conifers cling
Delicately, escaped the flows' polishing,
Cleaving thinly through the throes thunderous.

Never the grandeur of God more visible
Than the tornado torn walls composing
An ancient glacier carved cirque embracing
Spilling water sparkling, splashing, audible.

Welcome the washbowl — someday to be a bog
But today glinting gray, green, blue, sable
Against the grass and weeds edging shallows,
Holding minute grains against tomorrow
Across a marsh unimaginable,
The accidental stump and fallen log.

BIG SLIDE

Nature cleared the face of the monolith,
Tearing away awesome tonnage centuries
Had built into forested beauty with
Deft design of ferns, grasses, moss, and trees.

Much of what was believed mountain was flushed
From off its firm appearing foundation.
Not only plants, but rocks and thoughts were crushed
In a single day's grim emendation.

On other slopes sturdy flora compose
Gardens where all find a favorable place.
An inward force formed an angle of repose
But bare rock also mountain sides can grace.

Beauty destroyed and nothing left behind.
Beauty created of another kind.

SOUTH DIX

Summit rising every morning freshly
Painted by mists that drift and lift softly,
Reworking old materials in seasonal
Shades, ever changing still eternal.

Oval leaves shining green brightly bedeck
A meadow of rock by wind and fire blanched,
Yet rimmed with a mat of vegetation
Built on eons of endless circulation

Of dead mosses, lichens, leaves and roots mixed
With tiny minerals to catch moisture
Bunchberry and princess pine to nurture,
Spreading a coverlet at the feet of fir
Whose roots bulge above the earth showing strength
Derived from delving deep the duff beneath.

EAST DIX

Like the last in a line of skirmishers
Exposed on three flanks, but remaining firm,
You stand your ground against the persistent
Push of the profane who would a path pave

Across your wooded slopes to summits you protect
Not from the stresses of ancient adversity
But the short sighted who would scar your surface
And rudely blemish your aged beauty.

You would not crumble. You would not decline.
Long ago glacial scraping carved your slopes
Engendering your still developing soil.
Today's nearby highway lacks permanence.
Having shrugged off formidable attempts
To prove your endurance, your grace abides.

SADDLEBACK

Flaunting hues in an autumnal mixture hail
The becoming morning light. Haze-filtered
Red, orange, yellow and green, sun mottled,
Strike a harmony indifferent to detail.

Elderly trees sensing the season colder
Fling their congenial blanket atop
The range where gentle col yields to steeper slope,
Holding ten thousand years boulder to boulder.

Above the brook its spare seeping source leaks,
Before narrowing below to swift flow's noise,
A silent silver sheet o'er stony carpet
Of a sturdy singular chapelet
Serving unassuming summits equipoise
In a grand camaraderie of peaks.

BASIN

Following the tooth-marked trail of the beaver,
Man learned to timber and, later, treasure
The slopes and streams that feed pond and river
Across the surface of our floating sphere.

The shrubbiest tips of the most stunted trees
Surviving atop nature's prodigal
Provision signal aplenty for all,
Both down the slopes and down the centuries.

Mountain form, in an ocean of sky rising,
Ornaments but alters not nature's scheme,
Manifest in man's grasp, aggregating
Efforts enriching the poorest of men.

Sun, stars, wind, rain, climates cloudy and clear
Give to the growth of our garden grandeur.

WOLFJAW   (II)

Windblast blows down trees not to blow down trees
But only to be wind. Limbs lifted on air
Tug at trunks until their deepest roots tear,
Obeying nature's unyielding decrees.

Rain, vital plants and animals nourished,
Soaks soil beyond its capacity given
To absorb and soon begins to loosen
All. Forest crashes where all had flourished.

Such seeming loss will not last eternally.
The machinery that built these mountains
That we might find our bowers and our fountains
Restores the balance and builds new harmony.

We dimly see where today's fallen tree
Has its place in the order that's to be.

CLIFF

Halfway up a steep and verdurous slope
Brown-leafed birches with pungent balsams blend,
Not too distant tumbling waters wend
Across the frostinged forest's whitespread scope.

Weak but welcome sunlight dapples ridges, curved
Rainbow coated webs at limb tips sparkle,
Paw prints in the dusted grasses darkle,
Eye and ear and nose, all copiously served.

Such phenomenal beauty may be passing,
But it's not wasted when it simply stirs
A feeling that prompts us to stop and stare.
At times we need not know why nature's pleasing.
The joy we sense, for all we know, we share
With mouse and fox and deer and drowsy bear.

MARCY

Mountain noble matched to noble ministry
Through simple soil, rock, and plant congregate
Underlying joy through geometry
Gracious, slopes gathering grandeur consummate.

Every grain of soil, every massive rock
Speaks to us in patterns of spirit wrought.
Every fragile flower, every sturdy stock
Furthers forth invisible steps of thought.

Broadest base building to beauty's pinnacle,
Splitting clouds of exoteric blindness,
Highest of high peaks standing proud and humble,
Angled upward in a sky eternal,
Breaks a trail to nature's truest kindness,
A gorge can fill, should a mountain crumble.

GOTHICS

Grand three-peaked crest stark beauty radiates
To strike unsought the eye, the heart, the mind,
As rhythmic natural form ingeminates
An elevation of an inward kind.

Then from a choir angelic emanates
Harmony in every hour and season,
Splendid composition that illuminates
Gorges, slides and crags to the horizon.

A tree, a stream, a slide, a rock, a ridge,
Components in sublime concatenation,
A catechism on concinnous grace
Granted by divine artistry to bridge
The gorge dividing act from meditation
And raise the thought of man to heaven's face.

HOUGH

Warm sunshine halted the glacial advance.
Rain, clouds, fog, snow and wind shaped the flora.
Ages of dying flowers fed the future,
Leaving a laboratory and chapel
Embedded in a garden unsurpassed.

No where else is found the forest's fragrance.
Windstunted spruce and balsam scent rocky crops,
Yielding slopes to low bushes where globular
Bells bring blueberries gleaned by browsing bears.

Bright lambkill bursts in bloom, then shyly recedes,
Labrador tea waves forth its wooly leaves,
Urn shaped bells of leather leaf may adorn
Both a swampy bog and scabrous summit,
Burgeoning before the frosts of August.

ARMSTRONG

Your beauty forms a question yet unframed
For the eye to explore engendering thought
That longs for language, feelings to proclaim
What head beheld and heart alone had caught.

All seasons bring forth, brighten, and reveal
The earth's experience that we may know
Through nature's silent clock our own ordeal,
The stream's spring surge and shallow summer flow.

Our thoughts are rooted in the firmament
Of reason, reiterated in a blade
Of grass, a flower's bud, a fallen leaf.
Your language forges every sentiment
From visible appearance that will not fade,
Embowering heart and head once mute and deaf.

SKYLIGHT

A grand roof overlooking a grand gorge,
Vast recesses, suffers no scarcity
Of dancing water, rock, and light to forge
An intricate, sweet and sylvan purity.

The curvature of a summit gentle
Strewn with glacier spilled boulders erratic
Bordered by alpine meadow, fragrant, fragile,
Encompasses acres of open rock.

Light passes through you from whence and whereto?
We can only see but never explain
Beyond the laws we and you adhere to.
What the eye beholds stirs something in the brain

That wants to name the sweeping curve graceful
And find the bright alpine flowers restful.

BLAKE

Little birds, large birds in the high country
Spread across the slopes of the wooded mountain
On the duff, on the shrubs, on the tallest tree,
Visitors, feeding, breeding, not to remain.

Water brings the duck, the grebe, the heron
Wading, watchful, stepping solitary.
High above the hawk sights his prey whereon
He dives. Each succeeds. Colors, methods vary.

In the mixed forest, robins and wrens find foods.
High slopes harbor Hudsonian chickadee.
Each has it range, each range has its limits.
Diverse birds nurtured in abundant woods
Do not sort by size, but select company.
Sweet white throats join slate juncos at the summit.

HAYSTACK

The last leaves of the withered world cover
The forest floor down wooded slopes unhidden
By any canopy. Doddered trees hover
Darkening grey upon grey unbidden.

Your rugged peak broods watchful and wary
Over the gorge, the grey-green gorge, and clear
Purling streams carve a scarce covered quarry
Under the slate hued sky and rolling year.

After the autumn flush, the seeming doom
Of beauty, after all is harvested,
Hoarded, stacked and stored, after the harsh gloom
Of the browned off earth's frozen denial,
Then the sun rises on frosted summit,
Warrant of the covenant perennial.

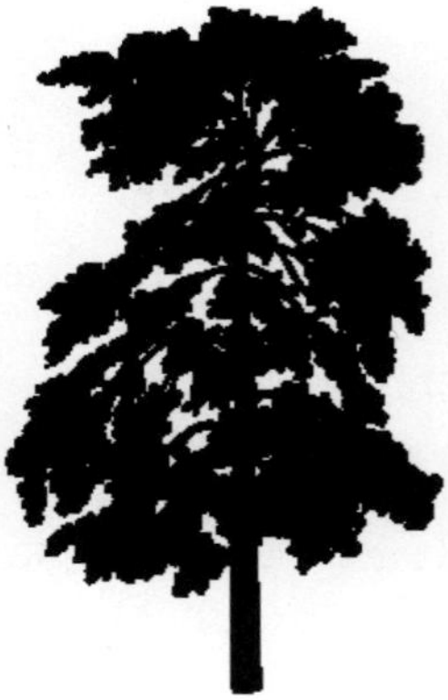

FORTY SIX NOTES

The notes that follow are intended as a glimpse into each of the forty-six peaks recognized by the ADK Forty-Sixers and originally believed to be over 4000 feet above sea level. More accurate measurements have shown a handful of those to be inaccurate and identified a couple of peaks overlooked. I stick with the Forty Sixers. The content of these notes is gleaned from several general sources and is widely known. The numbers following the names denote rank among the peaks and elevation

ALGONQUIN (2) 5114 Imagine Jacques Cartier coming upon the Algonquians and the Iroquois, as friendly neighbors along the St. Lawrence in the 16th century. Later when the Iroquois moved into central New York, they were to become rivals for hunting grounds. Boundary Peak was thought to be the divide, but that is one of many disputed origins for names. Neither tribe would have any need for the Artic alpine vegetation restoration developed from efforts of E.H. Ketchledge. The first recorded ascent was the Emmons party in 1837.

ALLEN (26) 4340 Picture a thunderous storm in 1869 that resulted in the avalanche into the lake of that name. Caught in that storm among others were a Boston minister, Frederick Allen, and his close friend and fellow minister, Joseph Twichell, who is later credited with suggesting the name. The summit is wooded.

ARMSTRONG (22) 4400 Thought to be the site of a legendary lead mine of the Indians, the peak has beautiful cliffs, densely wooded summit and a great ledge. A Plattsburgh lumberman owned the Totten and Crossfield Purchase, and his partner named the mountain for him. Local folk continued for some time to refer to it as Mountain Brook Hump.

BASIN (9) 4827 For some, the "crown jewel" for its great circular gorge, steep slopes and vast stand of virgin timber. On the first recorded ascent, Ed Phelps, told Colvin how his father -- Old Mountain Phelps -- had told him how he had named the mountain while viewing it from Tahawus with the artist Frederick Perkins. Think how few had seen it.

BIG SLIDE (27) 4240 Two slides -- in 1830 and 1856-- came down respectively the east and west slopes of the mountain. The slides showed no respect whatsoever for the political boundary dividing Keene from North Elba. One could easily infer that some soil today could easily be commingled.

BLAKE (43) 3960 Located appropriately next to Colvin, this peak commemorates the -- by all accounts -- modest, diligent man who was Colvin's chief assistant for the Survey and life-long friend, Mills Blake. His contribution to the success of creating the ADK park is recognized by historians, if not the general public.

CASCADE (36) 4098 Another of the abundant name changes, this mountain had been Long Pond Mountain for years. Nature and man intervened. Nature sent a avalanche that apparently added to the spit of land that turned the long pond into two smaller ones. An enterprising man came along and built a little hotel on the spot between the lakes and established within the hotel a post office named Cascadeville .

CLIFF (44) 3960 When you look at it, it hard to tell it's another of the "less than 4000' Club." The mountain practically shouts its name southward from its rugged face.

COLDEN (11) 4714 A small group guided by Lewis Elijah, son of the Abenaki Indian, Sabael, explored the iron ore veins in the area in 1826. They bought thousands of acres for tens cents an acre. Eventually the McIntyre Iron Works was established. One of its proprietors and a leader in the 1836 expedition was Judge Duncan McMartin, a man of considerable commitment to the region. Another in the group was Redfield who conferred the name Colden (one of their party and a one or two time visitor) on the lake. The mountain of the easterly side was to be Mc Martin. Somewhere along the way, Colden's name stuck to both.

COLVIN (39) 4057 Superintendent of the Adirondack Survey was not a desk job. Verplanck Colvin explored, surveyed and mapped the region for thirty-five years. Disputes over payments and title to records led to an incomplete mission in one sense. But no dispute ever existed over the enthusiasm and dedication Colvin lavished on the task. The Adirondack Park and Forest Preserve -- and all they mean to us -- cannot be thought about without his coming to mind.

COUCHSACHRAGA (46) 3820 If you cannot pronounce it, do not feel lonely; if you are not sure of the spelling, do not feel lonely; if you are not sure of its meaning do not feel lonely. Whether it is "winter habitation" or "beaver hunting ground" or "dismal wilderness" few are touchy about how to say "old Couchy."

DIAL (41) 4020 Another of our mountains with a name that has an "unsettled career" moving across at least two other peaks and carrying contradictory stories. A.B. Street wanted Nippletop to be Dial, Old Mountain Phelps objected to any city folk renaming his beloved mountains. Camel's rump became Noonmark . Only the names, not the mountains, moved.

DIX (6) 4857 Another governor. This one had quite an illustrious career as soldier in the War of 1812 and as a General in the Civil War. History credits him with persuading Maryland to remain neutral after Bull Run . He served as minister to France, U.S. Senator, Secretary of the Treasury. His name is on not only the mountain but the range. He probably would prefer not to have three peaks with his name.

DONALDSON (33) 4140 A man who spent years at the opening of the twentieth century researching and writing about the Adirondacks as a mostly convalescent resident of the Saranac region. He stayed to become a much beloved citizen serving on the village board. While some of his work has seen revision, he is still widely read and respected.

EAST DIX (42) 4012 A gracious companion to Dix, somehow overlooked in the naming processes, and not easily reached. Surely someone could think of a name that could grace this peak more gracefully than East something or other. Gracious!

EMMONS (40) 4040 Named for a man who taught at a small men's college in western Massachusetts as a botanist and conducted the New York state geological survey. His study of the "Taconic system" is said to have started the War of the Geologists!" No treaty is extant.

ESTHER (28) 4240 Try to imagine the percentage of people who visit Whiteface every year who have never heard of Esther -- the mountain -- to say nothing of the exuberant fifteen-year-old who climbed it way back when for the "sheer joy of climbing."

GIANT (12) 4627 This is the big one with a beautiful waterfall that everyone on Route 73 sees, stops at, and admires. Almost everything anyone's ever heard about or imagined the High Peaks to be confronts the inner and outer eye grandly.

GOTHICS (10) 4736 Colvin's account of his experience with ice, temperature, darkness, precipitous slides, lack of food, and the fearful noise, still managed to take note of the beauty of the moon on the "vast masses of ice dashing the abyss below." Contemplate the impression it made on him.

GRAY (7) 4840 All are encouraged to read Colvin's account of the "echo method" of triangulation for determining where he was in a drizzly fog as he searched to resolve the question of the sources of the Hudson River. He found the small body of water " in its minuteness and its prettiness, a veritable Tear-of-the-Clouds…"

HAYSTACK (3) 4960 A rather truly "nom de descriptive." So far there has not been a governor of that name, so the story of Old Mountain Phelps naming it is probably accurate. Ketchledge saw its forested slopes and Alpine summit as taking us to "ancient times."

HOUGH (23) 4400 Naming this mountain set almost as many feet scrambling as climbing it. But the titleholder was a native New Yorker who was to become known as the "Father of American Forestry" and was influential in the creation of the forest preserves.

IROQUOIS (8) 4840 Positioned as it is at the southern head of a several mile range and appropriately adjacent to Algonquin, this peak reminds us of the nation of people who inhabited so much of the region to the south and west of the area. Boundary Peak (too close to be classified separately by the Forty-Sixers) reminds us of how flexible the titles to Indian lands appear to have been.

LOWER WOLFJAW (30) 4175 One word, two word, one jaw or two. Such is the stuff of placing names on maps. What's recalled is the very real presence of wolves in the Adirondacks. Some say they've been extinct there for a century; some say they are only a greatly diminished presence but sighted occasionally. Most agree Noonmark is the place to view the profile.

MACOMB (21) 4405 A father and son both prominent in Adirondack history: the father for acquiring more than three and a half million acres at eight pence an acre at the western edge of the region after the Revolutionary War. The son, also Alexander, was a general in the War of 1812 and a hero at Plattsburgh who subsequently became commander-in-chief of the U.S. Army.

MARCY (1) 5344 Tahawus or Cloudsplitter are favored by some, but the historians say the scientists of Emmons party named it for the governor who supported their work. While the Troy lawyer and U.S. Senator who became governor in 1831 was not a hiker, he was a war veteran and had a distinguished career. Phelps called it "Mercy" unrelated.

MARSHALL (25) 4360 Robert Marshall, his brother George, and their guide, Herbert Clark were the first to climb "all the forty-six major peaks of the Adirondacks." Bob Marshall had a distinguished career in American forestry. The Forty-Sixers account of the naming of this mountain suggests the same degree of difficulty as climbing it.

NIPPLETOP (13) 4620 One blushes to recount the task of preserving the name of this peak by residents resisting the sensibilities of some summer visitors. If you can figure out how Haystack got its name, how much explication does this one need? Whatever one believes about the tales of a lost cave and other imaginative stirrings, it's a lovely peak.

NYE (45) 3895 Linked always as a "twin tramp" with its neighbor Street, this is the home of the "random scoot," as Old Mountain Phelps referred to hiking on trailless mountains. Despite its altitude as determined by later surveys, Nye has always been counted as one of the Forty Six

PANTHER (18) 4442 Unlike the wolf, the panther's total demise in the Adirondacks has always remained a slightly open question. Numerous sightings, even some kills, have continued to be reported. Clearly the old Adirondack mountain lion continues to inhabit at least the imagination.

PHELPS (32) 4161 Orson Schofield Phelps, colorful guide with the inclinations of the natural philosopher, namer of peaks, and voice of the area to many, by all accounts had a sense of joy about the Adirondacks that may remain unmatched. His vocabulary is sprinkled throughout Adirondack writings.

PORTER (38) 4059 Some summer residents blend well with the local folk. Noah Porter, a president of Yale, apparently was able to. He hiked and rowed and enjoyed the area. He climbed the mountain named for him when it was trailless.

REDFIELD (15) 4606 What must it have been like to be an apprenticed harness maker fascinated with the natural world? What must it have been like as a twenty-one year old to walk from Connecticut to Ohio in twenty-seven days to visit your mother, then walk back? What must it have been like to work your trade and spend every spare moment studying science? What must it have been like at age thirty-two to publish a theory on the paths of storms that was to become a classic in meteorology? And what must of it have been like to have been a member of the first group of scientists to have climbed and named the "High Peak of Essex"? William C. Redfield knew.

ROCKY PEAK RIDGE (20) 4420 Another mountain with an interesting series of name changes, this mountain stands as a fine example of how nature restores and renews after fiery devastation. Good work by conservation and county highway departments have also added some to the effort.

SADDLEBACK (17) 4515 Location, location, location. Situated between two of the highest and most spectacular of the peaks in the Great Range, Saddleback was often slighted by early reports.

SANTANONI (14) 4607 Most now agree the name is likely a corruption of the French for Saint Anthony of Padua filtered through the Abenaki Indians. No place is a finer example of the mixing of cultures and conflicting interests in the region.

SAWTEETH (35) 4100 Striking profiles arrest the attention whether human or mountainous. Imagine what must have occurred to create such geological formations. Consider how such silhouettes stir our imaginations.

SEWARD (24) 4361 Named for a graduate of Union College, who became governor and later Lincoln's secretary of state, now best remembered for his folly -- the purchase of the most vast wilderness in the U.S. -- Alaska.

SEYMOUR (34) 4120 A governor who actually hiked in and loved the Adirondacks. He headed the commission that laid the groundwork for the creation of the forest preserve. Horatio Seymour was a candidate for president of the United States. He lost that one to Ulysses S. Grant.

SKYLIGHT (4) 4924 Envision a few acres of open bedrock scarred with fissures and strewn with boulder erratics and rimmed with wind-dwarfed trees and delicate appearing alpine plants at almost 5,000 feet above sea level. Two men -- an artist and his guide -- viewed this from a nearby peak, taking particular note of the surface of a large rock projection suffused with light.

SOUTH DIX (37) 4060 Desolation, evidence of long past fire, was the dominant impression. Such a sight brought only a belittling set of notes and no distinctive appellation at time of the first ascent. Yet, listen to the rustle of the leaves in the wind on its slopes and it's a wild and wonderful place. Some think it deserves better. At least a name of its own.

STREET (31) 4166 Picture a somewhat scholarly young lawyer who becomes the state's law librarian and later head of the state library and at the same time an ardent writer about the Adirondacks. Also picture a shaggy, bearded north country guide. How delicious that their names should be forever linked by adjacent Adirondack peaks. How nicely they represent the range.

TABLETOP (19) 4427 The joy of a random scoot can still be experienced, but repeated scoots and surveyors and timbermen over generations engender herd paths, and conservationists eventually recognize the wiser course and designate accordingly. Down comes the canister and up goes the summit sign on an almost flat top.

UPPER WOLFJAW (29) 4185 What you perceive results from many factors, visual and otherwise. The scientist tends to see one thing; the artist perceives the same object somewhat differently. Both perceptions can occur in the same person observing the same object. No finer example can be found than the artistic surveyor and mapper of mountains who found himself on this one by mistake on its first recorded ascent.

WHITEFACE (5) 4867 Take away the elevator. Take away the weather observatory. Take away the road. Take away the chair lift. Take away the parking lots and restaurant. See this nearly solitary mountain rising to its lofty, rocky summit. Think about being impressed by the fact that this was the only high peak climbed on horseback and that most of the people who reached its summit were skiers and snowshoers. How would you feel if somebody suggested building a road to the top?

WRIGHT (16) 4580 Consider the consternation of a visiting writer worried about the efforts of the state to impose the names of politicians on the prominent peaks of the Adirondack Mountains, this vast and essentially remote region. Let a century pass. A Strategic Air Command bomber, on it way to a nearby air base, crashes on the summit, killing the four airmen on board. Their names are on a plaque at the site.

A BRIEF AFTERWORD

One summer's day, my wife Arlene and I went for a pleasant walk along the Boreas to the Hewitt Eddy. We carried our lunch along. We chose for our table a boulder at the end of a four or five rock path into the river that placed us far enough from the bank to be in the sunshine. Also among our accommodations was a large silver trunk of a blowndown, weathered Hemlock. Music to dine by was offered by the Boreas players. Our table was generously decorated.

On this large streamside piece of granite with a slender crevice, I noted growing from the crevice at least fifteen plant species including: trees (Cedar, Spruce, Maple) ferns, three bushes ... grasses, sedges, moss, wildflowers (lance leafed , daisy-like,) and lichens. My knowledge of plants is severely limited; heaven only knows how many I missed. All on a rock not larger than ten foot by ten foot in surface.

That made me think about the fragile hierarchy in the vastness of the Adirondacks.

Oh, that you would be altogether silent.
That for you would be wisdom.
Job 13: 5